sleep tight with
ANGELS
tonight

Lullabies, poems and prayers for bedtime

Original lyrics, poems and stories by **Mary Kay Beall**

Shawnee Press, Inc. &

1107 17th Avenue South • Nashville, TN 37212

www.shawneepress.com/songbooks

SB1037

About this book and CD...

Sleep Tight with Angels Tonight is designed to create a special interactive bonding experience for parent and child.

• Part One of the enclosed CD contains music and the spoken word which correspond to selected pages in the book. There are several "music only" sections in Part One designed for the parent to personally speak poems and words of comfort to the child.

This symbol ⊙ **30** is on the pages which correspond to track indexes on the CD. This will help you follow along for those sections on the CD which match pages in the book. The number at the top of this symbol is for Listening Tracks. The number at bottom is for Sing-along Tracks. A complete CD Track Index Listing is found on page 80.

• Part Two of the CD contains the same music as in Part One, but without the singing or spoken words, allowing the parent to sing along or read along to the entire music soundtrack for the child (using the corresponding printed material in the book).

• Bonus Material! A printable PDF file is included on the audio CD which includes information on the benefits of using music and lullabies for your child in the prenatal and infant stages of development. Research shows that reading to your infant (even while the child is in the womb) has far-reaching positive effects for the child's development and sense of security. Simply insert the CD into your computer and open the PDF file to view or print out the bonus material.

With beautiful illustrations, music and spiritual lyrics and scripture, **Sleep Tight with Angels Tonight** is designed to be a comforting and enriching experience for parent and child.

The Publisher

Sleep, My Baby, Sleep Tonight

Mary Kay Beall

William B. Bradbury

Sleep, my ba - by sleep to - night,

Sleep un - til the morn - ing light.

An - gels gath - er 'round to pray,

keep you safe 'til break of day.

Sleep, ba - by sleep,

Sleep, ba - by sleep.

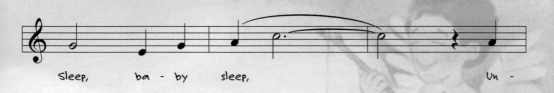

Sleep, ba - by sleep, Un -

til the break of day.

All Through the Night

Mary Kay Beall

Welsh folk melody

1. Sleep, my child, and peace at-tend thee
2. While the moon her watch is keep - ing

All through the night.
All through the night,

Guard - ian an - gels God will send thee
While the wear - y world is sleep - ing

All Through the night.
All through the night;

6

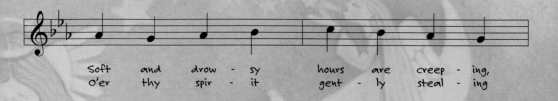

Soft and drow - sy hours are creep - ing,
O'er thy spir - it gent - ly steal - ing

Hill and dale in slum - ber sleep - ing.
Vis - ions of de - light re - veal - ing,

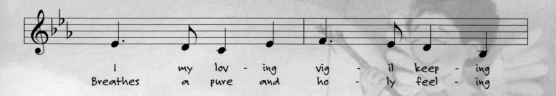

I my lov - ing vig - il keep - ing
Breathes a pure and ho - ly feel - ing

All through the night.
All through the night.

Sleep, baby, sleep,
Sleep, baby, sleep,
Sleep, baby, sleep,
Until the break of day.

I'd Like to Be an Angel

I'd like to be an angel
with silken feathered wings.
I'd spend my days and nights and noons
doing angel things.
I'd sing the songs that angels sing.
I'd dance the days away.
Then every night I'd flutter down
to hear the children pray.

Mary Kay Beall

"Lord, keep us safe this night,
Secure from all our fears;
May angels guard us while we sleep
Till morning light appears."

John Leland (1754-1841)

Parent can read this prayer while music plays

"I want to be an angel
and with the angels stand.
A crown upon my forehead...
a harp within my hand."

Urania Locke Bailey (1820-1882)

Parent can read poem while music plays

"The angels come to visit us know them

Parent can read quote while music plays

**and we only
when they are gone."**

George Eliot (1819-1880)

Day Is Done, My Child

Mary Kay Beall

Traditional Spiritual

1. Day is done, my child, day is done. Gone the
2. An - gels all a - round while you sleep, An - gels

sun, my child, gone the sun. Race is run, my child, race is
all a - round vi - gil keep. An - gels all a - round, night be -

run. Day is done, day is done.
gun, Day is done, day is done.

16

...and great will be your
children's peace.
Isaiah 54:13 NIV

"**Music is well said to be the**

speech of angels." Thomas Carlyle (1785-1881)

Now I lay me down to sleep.
I pray the Lord my soul to keep.
May angels gather in the night
and keep me safe 'till morning light.

Goodnight, dear Lord.
Please keep me safe
until this night is through.
Goodnight, big moon.
Goodnight, bright stars.
Goodnight, you angels, too.

Mary Kay Beall

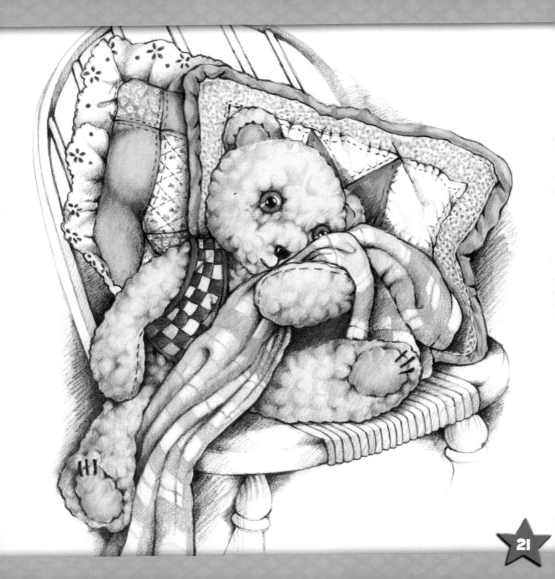

"We shall find peace. We shall hear
We shall see the

22

the angels,
sky sparkling with diamonds."

Anton Chekhov (1860-1904)

All Night, All Day

Mary Kay Beall

Traditional Spiritual

All night, all day
An - gels watch-in' o - ver me, my Lord.
All night, all day,
An - gels watch-in' o - ver me.

Fine

24

Went   down   to   the   val - ley   to   pray,

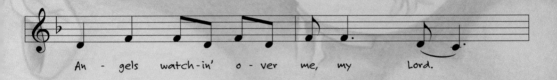

An - gels watch-in' o - ver me, my   Lord.

Prayed   all   night   and   prayed   all   day,

D.C. al Fine

An - gels watch-in' o - ver me.

"All God's angels come to us disguised."

James Russell Lowell (1819-1891)

Angels All Around My Bed

Mary Kay Beall

Traditional Spiritual

1. An - gels all a - round my bed, Al - le - lu - ia! An - gels all a - round my bed, Al - le - lu - ia! 2. Gold - en

harps, and sil - ver wings, Al - le -
(3.) with me through the night, Al - le -

lu - ia! Gold - en
lu - ia! An - gels

harps, and sil - ver wings, Al - le - lu -
with me through the night, Al - le - lu -

1
ia!

2
3. An - gels ia!

29

THE GOODNIGHT ANGEL

It was time to go to sleep but Mikey couldn't.
He knew he should... but he couldn't.
Mike was waiting. He was lying very still...
waiting.

Mikey was listening. He was lying very, very
still...listening.
He knew he just couldn't go to sleep...yet.

But then he heard a sound... a fluttering sound.
And a soft little voice whispered in his ear,
"Mikey, it's me. I'm here.
Close your eyes and go to sleep."

Mikey took a deep, deep breath
and smiled a big smile
and closed his eyes
and whispered back,
"I was waiting for you!"

And the Goodnight Angel smiled back
and settled in for the night.

Mary Kay Beall

"...God commands the angels to guard you in
they shall support you lest

Parent can read scripture while music plays

all your ways. With their hands
you strike your foot against a stone."

Psalm 91:11-12

"God and all angels sing the world to sleep."

Wallace Stevens (1879-1955)

"There is joy in the presence of the angels"

Luke 15:10 NASB

"The reason angels can fly is because they take themselves lightly."

G. K. Chesterton - (1874-1936)

Parent can read while music plays

Lullaby and Goodnight

Mary Kay Beall

Johannes Brahms

sun - shine and play, Dream a -

way, dream a - way. Set your

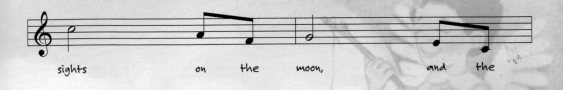

sights on the moon, and the

morn - ing will come soon.

39

Twinkle, Twinkle, All Night Long

Mary Kay Beall

French folk melody

Twin-kle, twin-kle, all night long While I sing my sleep-y song. When I see the morn-ing sun, Lit-tle star, your twin-kling's done. Twin-kle, twin-kle, all night long While I sing my sleep-y song.

Dream of sunshine and play,
Dream away, dream away.
Set your sights on the moon,
And the morning will come soon.

Dear Lord, I thank you for the day
and for the peace of night,
and while I sleep, I know You, Lord,
will guard my child tonight.

May angels come with silver wings
To give us all sweet dreams,
While moonbeams dance and planets prance
And to you my love sings.

While morning light
stays away tonight,
tomorrow, the sun drops in.
Amen.

Mary Kay Beall

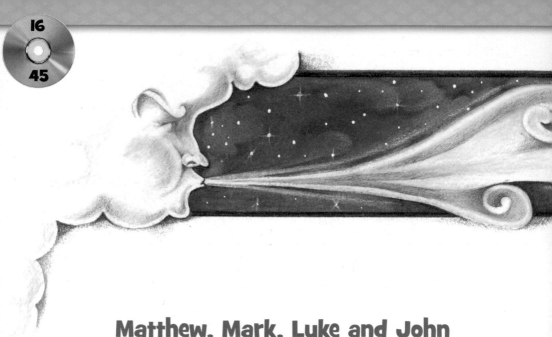

Matthew, Mark, Luke and John
Bless the bed that I lie on.
Bless the darkness soft as fleece.
Bless the silent sound of peace.
Bless the roof above my head.

Parent can read poem while music plays

Bless the blanket o'er me spread.
Bless me as I sleep tonight.
Bless me 'till the morning's light.

Based on 'A Candle in the Dark'
by Thomas Ady (17th century)

One Angel

Mary Kay Beall

English folk melody

At night when I have prayed my

prayer and dark has set - tled ev - 'ry -

where, I know an an - gel is hov - 'ring

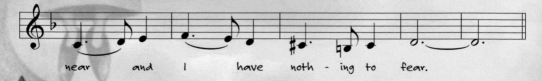

near and I have noth - ing to fear.

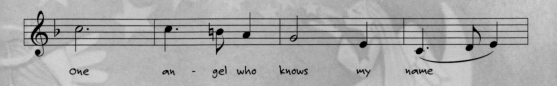

One an - gel who knows my name

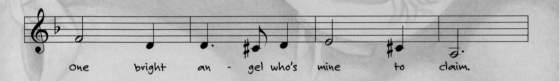

One bright an - gel who's mine to claim.

One an - gel in snow - y white to

keep me safe all thru the night.

Four bright angels I can see, Four bright
One to shoo away my fears.
One to pray an

angels watching me.
One to dry my midnight tears.
never quit. One to keep the candle lit.

Mary Kay Beall

49

I've Never Seen an Angel

I've never seen an angel
but that's because they're shy.
I've never seen an angel
but I know when one's near by.
I've never seen an angel
but when I'm fast asleep
I know an angel's watching...
but I'll never, ever peep!

Mary Kay Beall

Parent can read poem while music plays

**Praise the LORD, you His angels,
you mighty ones who do His bidding,
who obey His word.**

Psalm 103:20 NIV

Parent can read scripture while music plays

Sometimes I Feel
There's an Angel Close By

Mary Kay Beall

Traditional Spiritual

1. Some - times I feel there's an an - gel close by,
2. Some - times I hear an - gels whis - per my name,

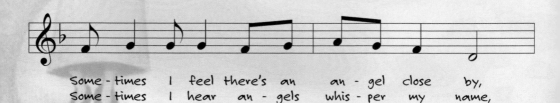

Some - times I feel there's an an - gel close by,
Some - times I hear an - gels whis - per my name,

Some - times I feel there's an an - gel close by, when
Some - times I hear an - gels whis - per my name, when

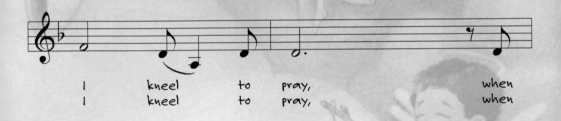

I kneel to pray, when
I kneel to pray, when

I kneel to pray.
I kneel to pray.

"I see the moon. The moon
God, bless the moon

sees me.
and God bless me!"
                    Anonymous

Two Little Angels

Two little angels flying through the night,
Two little angels with crowns of gold

Parent can read poem while music plays

Two little angels in gowns of white.
Happy to know they will never grow old.

Mary Kay Beall

...Children are a reward from Him.

Psalm 127:3 NIV

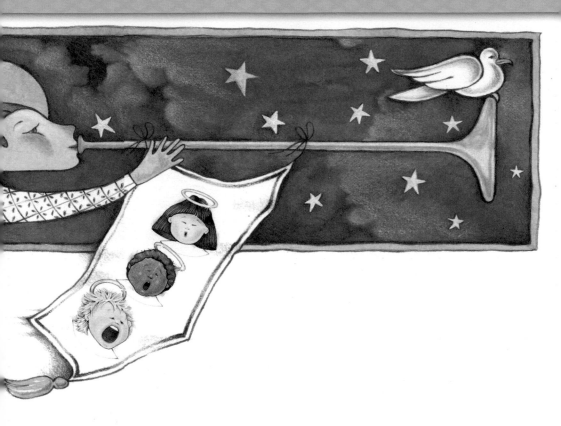

This Little Star of Mine

Mary Kay Beall

Traditional

This lit-tle star of mine, I'm gon-na let it shine. This lit-tle star of mine, I'm gon-na let it shine. This lit-tle star of mine, I'm gon-na let it shine. Let it shine, let it shine, let it shine.

The **LORD** watches over you— the **LORD**
is your shade at your right hand;
the sun will not harm you by day,
nor the moon by night.
The **LORD** will keep you from all harm—
He will watch over your life;
the **LORD** will watch over your coming and going
both now and forevermore.

Psalm 121: 5-8 NIV

Parent can read scripture while music plays

THE TWO FOOLISH ANGELS

Two little angels were racing across the sky
to see who could fly the fastest.
But they were careless.
Suddenly one of the angels
caught his wing on the corner of a star
and the other angel slammed right into him
and caught his wing too.

When the two little angels finally got loose
they tried to fly but they couldn't.
Each of them had a torn wing.
Instead of going up they went down
down
down
down
all the way to the earth.

They landed, "Thump! Thump!" in a grassy field.
How would they get home to heaven, they wondered.
What were they going to do?
Who ever heard of an angel who couldn't fly?
But then, one of the little angels had an idea.
"It only takes TWO wings to fly.
Between us, we still have TWO good wings.
If we put our arms around each other
maybe we could fly back to heaven together."

And that's just what they did.
When the Head Angel heard their story
he knew they had been foolish
but he decided they had learned a lesson.
He repaired their torn wings
and that night both of those little angels
flew down to earth to watch over a sleeping child.

Mary Kay Beall

67

Rockabye, rockabye, baby so dear
Rockabye, rockabye, nighttime is near
Rockabye, rockabye, time to count sheep
Rockabye, rockabye, sleep, baby, sleep.

Mary Kay Beall

Parent can read this poem while music plays

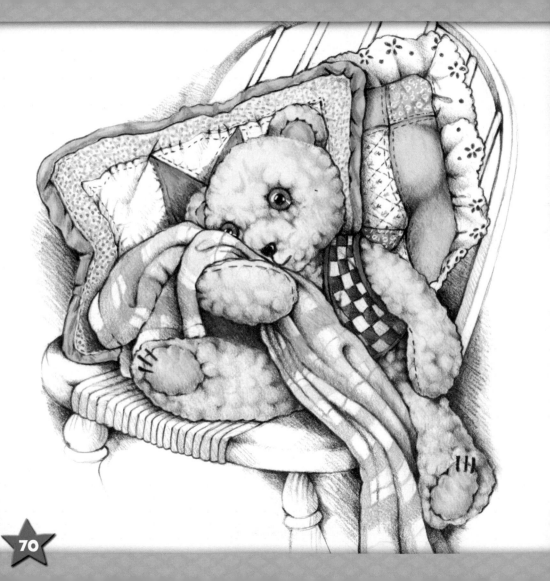

As a father has compassion on his children, so the LORD has compassion on those who fear Him...

Psalm 103: 13 NIV

Parent can read this scripture while music plays

Sleepytime's Calling

Mary Kay Beall

Stephen Foster

Sleep - y - time's call - ing   at close of day.

Stars bright a - bove you and moon-beams at   play.

Time now for dream - ing...   time now to spare.

Sail off to dream - land and spend the night   there.

Sleep - y eyes close   now   lulled by a song.

What could be sweet - er   as   night comes a - long?

Sleep - y eyes close   now.   Noth - ing to fear.

I'll be be - side you 'till morn - ing is here.

73

"See, I am sending an angel ahead of you to guard you along the way..."

Exodus 23:20 NIV

Parent can read this scripture while music plays

Lullaby, Little One

Mary Kay Beall

Irish folk melody

1. Lul - la - by, lit - tle one,
2. Lul - la - by, lit - tle one,

loo - lee, loo - lay.
loo - lee, loo - lay.

Hear the Night whis - per, "Good -
Hear the Night stars call - ing from

bye!" to the Day.
far, to far a - way.

Lul - la - by,   lit - tle   one,
Lul - la - by,   lit - tle   one,

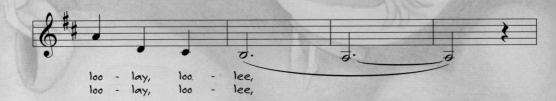

loo - lay,   loo - lee,
loo - lay,   loo - lee,

Climb   on   a   moon - beam   and
All   through   the   dark of night, you'll be

sail   off   with   me.
safe   as   can   be.

Our Father in heaven, hallowed be Your name.
Your kingdom come, Your will be done
on earth as it is in heaven.
Give us today our daily bread.
Forgive us our debts,
as we also have forgiven our debtors.
And lead us not into temptation,
but deliver us from the evil one,
for Yours is the kingdom
and the power and the glory forever.
Amen.

Matthew 6: 9-13 NIV

Parent can read this scripture while music plays

CD Track Index

Part One - Listening Tracks:
1) Sleep, My Baby, Sleep Tonight
2) All Through the Night
3) Sleep, My Baby – reprise
4) I'd Like to Be an Angel
5) Lord, Keep Us Safe This Night
6) Day Is Done, My Child
7) Now I Lay Me Down to Sleep
8) All Night, All Day
9) Angels All Around My Bed
10) The Goodnight Angel
11) God Commands the Angels
12) Lullaby and Goodnight
13) Twinkle, Twinkle, All Night Long
14) Lullaby and Goodnight – reprise
15) Dear Lord, I Thank You
16) Matthew, Mark, Luke and John
17) One Angel
18) Four Bright Angels
19) I've Never Seen an Angel
20) Sometimes I Feel There's an Angel Close By
21) I See the Moon
22) Two Little Angels
23) This Little Star of Mine
24) The Lord Watches Over You
25) The Two Foolish Angels
26) Rockabye, Rockabye
27) Sleepytime's Calling
28) Lullaby, Little One
29) Our Father in Heaven

Part Two - Sing-along Tracks:
30) Sleep, My Baby, Sleep Tonight
31) All Through the Night
32) Sleep, My Baby – reprise
33) I'd Like to Be an Angel
34) Lord, Keep Us Safe This Night
35) Day Is Done, My Child
36) Now I Lay Me Down to Sleep
37) All Night, All Day
38) Angels All Around My Bed
39) The Goodnight Angel
40) God Commands the Angels
41) Lullaby and Goodnight
42) Twinkle, Twinkle, All Night Long
43) Lullaby and Goodnight – reprise
44) Dear Lord, I Thank You
45) Matthew, Mark, Luke and John
46) One Angel
47) Four Bright Angels
48) I've Never Seen an Angel
49) Sometimes I Feel There's an Angel Close By
50) I See the Moon
51) Two Little Angels
52) This Little Star of Mine
53) The Lord Watches Over You
54) The Two Foolish Angels
55) Rockabye, Rockabye
56) Sleepytime's Calling
57) Lullaby, Little One
58) Our Father in Heaven